This book is dedicated with great appreciation
to my friends Barb and Judy, who pray for me.

Edited by Aileen Andres Sox
Designed by Dennis Ferree
Art by Kim Justinen
Typeset in 14/18 Weiss

ISBN: 0-8163-1183-8

94 95 96 97 98 • 5 4 3 2 1

Teddy's Terrible Tangle

By Linda Porter Carlyle   Illustrated by Kim Justinen

Pacific Press Publishing Association
Boise, Idaho
Oshawa, Ontario, Canada

ell me about your new job, Uncle Jack," I say. I climb up beside him on the couch.

Uncle Jack looks proud. "I'm going to be a repairman for the phone company," he says.

"Do you get to ride in a big white truck?" I ask. "Do you have a belt full of tools?"

Uncle Jack laughs. "Yes and yes," he answers. "Do you want me to tell you a little bit about how telephones work?" he asks.

nod my head. "Oh yes," I say.
"Come look," says Uncle Jack, "there is a wire that runs from your telephone to the wall."

"I know," I say. "I can see it."

Uncle Jack smiles. "That wire goes through the wall and outside the house. It goes either to a tall pole, or it goes underground, where it joins lots of other wires from lots of other people's telephones. And do you know where all those wires go?" he asks.

I shake my head.

hey go to a big computer. When you pick up your telephone and dial a number—like when you call Grandpa—
the computer in our town sends your call to a computer in
Grandpa's town. And that computer sends your call to
Grandpa's telephone."

I look at Uncle Jack in surprise.

t's a complicated system," Uncle Jack says. "But it works very well unless something happens to one of the lines. A storm could knock down one of the big telephone poles. Or someone digging in the wrong place could cut some of the underground wires."

Then you go fix them, Uncle Jack?" I ask. "You're a wire fixer?"

Uncle Jack laughs. "That's right," he answers. "That's just what I am. I'm a wire fixer."

h, no! Come quickly!" Mama calls from the living room.

I run to see what is the matter. There is Teddy, all tangled up in Mama's yarn. He is kicking and rolling. I don't know if he's having fun or if he's scared. I rush to pick him up.

"What a terrible tangle!" Mama exclaims.

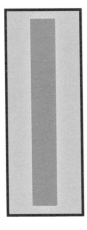

giggle. Teddy looks funny. He *has* made a terrible mess. I start to unwind him.

Mama sighs. "I guess I'll have to be a lot more careful about where I leave my yarn," she says.

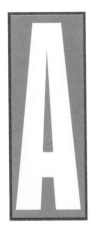re you all ready for bed?" calls Papa. "Did you brush your teeth and get a drink and go to the bathroom?"

"Yes," I call back. "I'm all ready."

Papa puts down the newspaper and comes down the hall to my bedroom. "Well, let's pray," he says. We kneel down beside my bed.

 don't need a wire to talk to God," I say.

"What?" asks Papa.

"I don't need a wire like a telephone does," I say.

apa laughs. "It would be awful if we needed a wire to be connected to God! Our earth is spinning through space. In a few minutes, everybody's wires would be all tangled up and broken! That would be a worse mess than the one Teddy made this afternoon," he says.

apa puts his arm around my shoulders. "Isn't it wonderful that we can be connected to God any time and anywhere? He can always hear us."

"Even if all the telephone poles fall down," I say.

"Even if all the telephone poles fall down."

od can hear me when I pray, in the night and in the day.

I don't always bow my head. Sometimes I talk to Him under my bed.

Parent's Guide

Share the Privilege of Prayer With Your Child

Through prayer, we have the private telephone number (so to speak) of the King of the Universe. Here are some simple ways to teach your child about prayer.

❖ A child learns naturally about prayer when she lives with parents who pray. Let her hear and see you praying at times like these—before meals, at the start of your day, at the end of your day, before and after family worship, whenever you need God's help or want to thank Him for something He has done for you. Remember what it was like to be little, and don't make your young children sit through long family prayers.

❖ When your child shows an interest in prayer, have him repeat phrases after you. Again, keep these prayers short. As your child grows older, he can pray more and more on his own. You can prompt his thoughts before prayer by saying things like, "What do you want to thank God for today?" "Maybe you would like to talk to God about the trouble you're having with your friend."

❖ Keep a family prayer journal or calendar. Record your requests and remember them in prayer. Keep track of God's answers as well.

❖ Tell stories about answered prayer. Read some of Jesus' prayers and the prayers of other Bible characters.

❖ Remember that God answers prayers Yes, No, or Wait.

Sometimes He answers in ways we do not at all expect. And, He doesn't force people to choose to do the right thing. That means that our prayers for other people to change do not always result in the answer we want. Nevertheless, God tells us to pray for each other and promises that when good people pray, great things happen (see James 5:16).

❖ Teach your child that he can tell God anything. Even if he is angry at God, he can pray about it! God cares about the slightest thing that worries us. He is never too busy to listen or to act in our behalf.

❖ Ask God to help your home be one in which prayer is as natural as eating and sleeping. He will prove His promise over and over again, "Ask and you will receive, and your joy will be complete" (John 16:24, NIV).

Linda Porter Carlyle and Aileen Andres Sox

Books by Linda Porter Carlyle

I Can Choose
A Child's Steps to Jesus

God and Joseph and Me
Rescued From the River!
Grandma Stepped on Fred!
Max Moves In
Cookies in the Mailbox
Beautiful Bones and Butterflies

No Olives Tonight!
Happy Birthday Tomorrow to Me!
No Puppy Food in the Garden
Red and Purple on My Feet
Teddy's Terrible Tangle
My Very, Very Best Friend